Personal Science

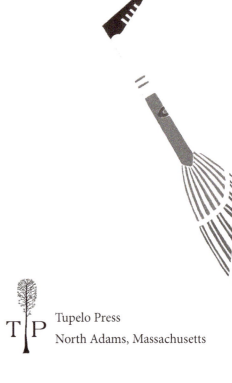

Tupelo Press

North Adams, Massachusetts

# Personal Science

LILLIAN-YVONNE BERTRAM

Library of Congress Cataloging-in-Publication Data available upon request.
ISBN: 978-1-936797-91-2

Cover and text designed by Josef Beery.
Cover art: Untitled, from the Greenheads series (2005).
Gouache and pencil on paper. Copyright © 2017 Laylah Ali.
Courtesy of the artist and Paul Kasmin Gallery.

First paperback edition: January 2017.

The epigraph is from *Homo Narrans: The Poetics and Anthropology of Oral Literature* by John D. Niles (University of Pennsylvania Press, 2010).

Tupelo Press
P.O. Box 1767, North Adams, Massachusetts 01247
Telephone: (413) 664–9611 / editor@tupelopress.org / www.tupelopress.org

Tupelo Press is an award-winning independent literary press that publishes fine fiction, nonfiction, and poetry in books that are a joy to hold as well as read. Tupelo Press is a registered 501(c)(3) nonprofit organization, and we rely on public support to carry out our mission of publishing extraordinary work that may be outside the realm of the large commercial publishers. Financial donations are welcome and are tax deductible.

**ART WORKS.**
arts.gov

Supported in part by an award from the National Endowment for the Arts

*for Mike Lynch*

# Contents

Homo narrans: *that hominid who not only has*
*succeeded in negotiating the world of nature,*
*finding enough food and shelter to survive, but also*
*has learned to inhabit mental worlds that pertain*
*to times that are not present and places that are*
*the stuff of dreams.*
*It is through such symbolic mental activities that*
*people have gained the ability to create themselves*
*as human beings and thereby transform the world*
*of nature into shapes not known before.*

— John D. Niles, from *Homo Narrans*

# Personal Science

# A little tether

A self being an object,        I can construct

the object I am trying to get to

Refer to the page

But when left, the page fades to pinks and yellows

To say the hammer was applied to the limb

to force breaking

is to say there was a wheel

Remember the wheel? Some said there wasn't any heart in it

Or, there was excess heart

Those medieval-*uns* were *currr-aaazzy*

The thing is just what's said

The line I try to get to

There are rules even for dreams

The cars are always cars I've driven

The men men I've known

**Legends like these I keep keeping**

*you are running away on a hot night,*     scraping the skin

off nectarines, lying on my bed when that loose skirt

you wear crosses the line he drew in marker

down the middle of the headboard, the line

he made with the heat of his hands

the night before our wedding

made of my neck a bottle

then ran me down the alley in nothing but

a ghostwhite t-shirt & panties. Learn to breathe

in a jar.

        In the rain steaming off the iron fire escape,

you say *this night smells of rust & oranges*

that our eyes cup lozenges of small light,

& in the rush of trains passing remote

under east liberty   *sliberty*   tracks tracking

between good town & bad town,

in the nightlong hum of riddance

I always hear a shoulder coming

to pop my doorchain from its lock

*I'm watching us*

        wave our vanishing
cigarettes
      out your window
   shouting that we hate
      the rich but love the money.
We mash & spin
         Nas & Chaka
      *I'mmmmmeverywommaaannnnn*
        *lifesabitchuntilyadiiiiieeeeeeee*
  & plan what we'll angle from the dumpster
   below: bricks, bike with busted seat
wood broken from a table
        but good enough for bed slats
   —moving days and the glossy
x-ray of your wrist
         split in two shines
   hangs still on the wall
      fractured as the moon
seen through plastic toy binoculars.
    I crook my arm,
  imitate your skeleton dangling
    over the edge of the bathtub
      the night 5F thought he was killing you,
her fist knocking against the wall,
      your head buzzing like the wasp
  you could never ignore
      crawling in circles
   at the bottom of a paper bag—*Stacey*
you shrieked over him, *you've got some nerve.*
      *I can always hear you breathing through*
  *this goddamn wall, little girl.*

*when we lie*

with    the    wolves    we    cheeks
crimson

in bluedark bluedark    we

cheeks underfoot

face  up  underside  the  princes  the

princes!

take  us,  print  us,  the  princes
make print of us

the  princes  does  us,  fat  tricks  us,

ribs the princes

was sure left print no night

*oh relieving* we cheeks hum undone

*when the city was ours,*     before you left

you said *I feel kind of lost when not on one of the coasts* so you put your hand between your legs & got high for weeks. your apartment, you said, *was too short, too hot*, it came on like *a sex in a boat* you said, *a fell asleep. here—go through my clothes—take what you want.* I said *I wish you blacked out against the sky, you know. unfuckable. and don't ever let a man fuck you up against an air-conditioner* I told you, *& don't ask me why, just don't be the kabob on a shish, all skin & girl, ass against some window.* it was you who said *get over yourself, it's love or bust, love or bust.* it was you who said *we are few & far between.* when you were ready to go I said *you better write me or I'll break your teeth.* we thought about going up to the roof a last time, to where night came on us like a bullet.

## 8    *Homo narrans* (turkey)

A rabbit is lying on the ground beneath a bush, grooming itself. I look again & next to the rabbit lies a fox. The two appear to be talking. The fox looks over its shoulder at me, as if to say, or it does say, *look, I'm not going to do anything.*

Behind us comes a large turkey & as we walk away from the turkey, the turkey begins to hurry up. The turkey's pace frightens me. All attempts to shoo the turkey away are failing, & now the turkey makes like the turkey wants to bite. I try to push the turkey away again, this time harder, but I worry about hurting the turkey & I find I cannot harm an animal I do not understand.

Now it seems us or the turkey. I do not know who throws the first stone. I give him my stone to throw but under the condition he does not throw it directly at the turkey's head. I turn my back and walk out of the grove. What        happens        next        I        cannot        say.

In the hotel garden I bend over my hands and count out the pills. I am worried I will not have enough pills. A man walks over and because he looks like the stud on the cover of a romance novel—not too dark but not too light—I figure he's the gardener. But it's the way he demands, like a policeman, that I do what he says and hand over the pills. He disappears.

The next day I harass the front desk clerk about the man. I yell at her about the pills. I shriek that he robbed me until my mouth gets frothy. She smiles as I call her names and insult her hair but still she just smiles then tells me that the man is gone. In the garden he was distracted by a bird and caught himself on the chainsaw, nearly in half. To prove it she points out to the blood spray on the garden's wooden fence.

## Cerebrum corpus monstrum

Nothing to be preserved
By the idea of paradise.

Take this pistol.

The old dog's ashes taken home in a cedar box.

Take this blindfold.

The warbler with the cinched wing won't take
From your handful of seeds.

Shoot into the crowd.

To feel the heart, you must
Put your hand in it.

♂

Your brother moves upslope in spring
Taken like broken water by grief for his dead.

Fabric into and out of this world. Put your hand
In it & give dearness to another.

Your brother makes a deal: To remember only the smell
Of chestnuts roasting in the aged plaza.

To live in smoke. To bed women only
In winter.

To send them off at the first of weather's breaking,
At the brute chatter of robins outside the east window.

♂

Two dead birds on Monday morning
& a shadow takes shape in the backseat of the car.

When you move to put your hand in it, to wipe it free:
An almost-full moon corners the afternoon sky

& a dog and a woman walking together
Become one deer crossing the road.

The barn swallow loops in circles around your ankles:
Throw down these sticks & read them.

☌

Forget the holidays, Good Friday & Easter,
& the insipid barn swallow, its blue upperparts

Shining. Alone on a road through Texas, following
The dips of a hawk you let the car weave across lanes

& nothing happened but the hawk kept flying away.
Though it was infinite & became but hallucination
You bear all this.

o⚲

You learn to pattern everything: the deer
At the far end of the field at dusk,

The grackle song & quick licks
Of the cat's bath, even the noontime raising

Of the blinds has its known motion.

You call up your brother without a thought
As to what you might say.

*Tell me something true about the two of us.*

When you reach into your purse
You touch last night's underwear.

*All we are unable to become becomes us.*

When your brother thinks you haven't
Got a chance he will still tell you *good luck.*

Even the slow biting of yet another man's neck,
The force of your thrusts, becomes you—outrun.

⚬

When I speak to my brother I ask him of premonition.
*Why not buy the ticket that will bring you fortune?*

*To stir your hand in deep strong water is something I'd rather*
*Not deal with.*

He asks what is new & I say *an unlucky eastern wind* or
*The terrible treefull of house finches.* I tell him *psychic unease.*

*Sounds like procrastination* he says. *You should cultivate*
*A more productive trait.*

*Take tenacity, for instance.*

⚯

Take this wet hair on the sheet.
Take this spillage.
Take this damp yawn against the nape of a neck.
Take the obscene light of the lit street.
Take these early birds and
Take this pistol to them.
Take this piece of gold.

I take this pistol.
I take this thorny briar.
I take this finger
Pointing like a pistol
& put it in my mouth.

I wet it all.

Give me back my gold.

♂

I am at my best on the nights of a sanguine moon
So pregnant

I reach up & put my hands in it, peel my fingers through
A moon that smells of two bodies taken, spilled, & drying

On our chins as we sleep. When I speak to my brother
About the disturbances of spring, the woodchucks

Scurrying at the wheels of my bicycle, he tells me
That each year he loses women to gentler cities.

I say that my love is sick with the future and as he dims
I too, dim in that way the moon grows our bodies heavier

At low tide. My brother says that this is the nature:

*One entangled particle affects the other.*

*It is the reason why we are alive and a door we reach to open is not.*

She checked the forecast. She checked it again. She checked the local forecast, then the national. She checked the forecast from east to west. A chance of snow in the Rockies, twelve or more inches over seven thousand feet. A nor'easter churning a hundred miles off Nova Scotia that could deliver something, or nothing but some sputtering flurries. She checked the forecast on the computer. Then she went to the kitchen and checked the forecast on her smartphone as she walked down the hall. While looking at the screen on her phone, at the graphic of a cloud partly covering the sun, her shoulder sharply glanced off the molding in the kitchen doorway.

♂

She checked the forecast a month out. Two months out. It was November. She checked the forecast into March. She checked the airport forecasts; she thought those forecasts were more accurate. She checked the ocean forecast, the forecast in the turbulent zones. She rechecked next week's forecast. She googled Italy's typical climate. She checked that day's forecast for Italy. It was in Celsius and this frustrated her. She checked the forecast at the Milan airport, then at JFK. She thought about e-mailing her brother, asking him what the weather was like in Milan in March, what she should pack, but she didn't. She checked the local forecast again. She looked through the blinds out the window at the soggy lawn and leafless street. Suddenly she remembered a package of breakfast sausage that had been in the freezer for months and was, last she checked, completely frost-bitten. She got up to throw it out.

⚮

And if there was a terrorist on the plane, what would she do? Would she alert someone to something suspicious? Would she

see something, say something? The phenomenon of assuming
that other people who are present will be the first to initiate some
sort of intervening action is sometimes called "Genovese" syn-
drome, named after Kitty Genovese who was stabbed to death
on a street in Queens in 1964 and in full view and earshot of
no less than thirty-eight neighbors. She knew that in the field of
organizational behavior, this was also called the "bystander ef-
fect" or "diffusion of responsibility," a situation that, in the field of
management, made it very difficult for people to effectively work
together in groups. She was twenty-eight. Kitty was stabbed to
death at the age of twenty-eight. Would she be brave, looking
for a moment to leap and tackle? With her left hand she reached
over and squeezed the bicep of her right arm, just to see what
kind of shape it was in. She thought that if confronted, if need be,
she could beat a man to death. But could she reason with a ter-
rorist? Would she and a terrorist even speak the same language,
or would they have to communicate only by looks? Could she
convince a terrorist to abdicate his action just by a look? Were
her eyes, was her look, special enough to give a terrorist pause?
Or would her breath squeeze her so tight that she became just a
face? Or some keyboard strokes—the third digit of a three-digit
number.

♂

The first hull loss of a Boeing 747 was Pan Am Flight 93 in 1970.
Having been hijacked in Brussels and detoured to Beirut to
eventually land in Cairo, the large plane was ultimately blown
up on the tarmac. A hull loss, she read, is the total destruction
of the plane, or when a plane has to be written off completely
due to damage. Just like a totaled car, she thought. Just like a
totaled car. Such accidents were not common. Planes were rou-
tinely damaged and subjected to the stress of pressurization and

decompression and planes were routinely fixed and maintained, their hulls prolonged. Total hull loss was rare, but when it did happen, such incidents were catastrophic.

♂

Just before they crashed into a house a few miles from the airport in February 2009, the pilots of the Newark–Buffalo Colgan Air Flight 3407 noticed the buildup of ice on the wings. Determined not to be a factor in the crash, icing conditions in Buffalo were typical for February. She knew how icy Buffalo could be, how suddenly wintry mix could channel over the city. It was an unpredictable place to live and she had lived there. Freshman year there had been thundersnow in the morning and by noon the school was sending everyone home. By the time she had arrived, hours later, her jeans were frozen from her knees to the cuffs she let drag on the ground. The jeans stayed standing where she left them on the porch, where her mother forced her to step out of them before coming inside the house.  In chatting about the co-pilot's head cold, the two pilots violated the rules for non-essential banter in the cockpit below 10,000 feet, an altitude that, she assumed, more or less corresponded to take-offs and landings. Neither the captain, who out of 3,379 flight hours had flown 109 as captain of this kind of aircraft, or the co-pilot, who had flown 772 of her 2,200 hours on the Q400, noticed the sudden drop in the plane's speed. They were, it seemed, distracted. This she could understand. It was cold and dark, the co-pilot's nose had been running. Her cross-country flight the day before probably hadn't helped. She might have been thinking of getting a new jacket. Maybe a new bra.

♂

And then the plane experienced, in aviation terms, a deep stall. Unrecoverable, she had read. She thought of her brother, of when they were children, of how they used to make paper airplanes to pass the time. They would fold and then sail the planes from the top of the stairs into the kitchen, or off the back porch into the yard if the day was warm and calm. The paper planes would glide up, up, and then slowly, pitching upwards, they would slow down and then start to roll, yaw, and spin haphazardly to the ground. Some, with all sorts of creases pressed into the wings, achieved no lift and nosed straight into the ground. The ones that went the furthest, she recalled, were those that caught the air quickly, gliding through it and then, as they lost speed and angled downward, flying low for a moment and then nosing up. They floated through the air on a mild sine wave before striking the kitchen windows.

♂

To recover from a stall, she read, was actually quite simple. In the event of a stall, which is a lack of enough speed to maintain wing lift, to recover one must point the nose of the plane down and apply thrust to regain the speed required for lift. Think of a bird, she told herself, beating its wings as it directs itself toward the ground, and soaring back up. She thought she could conjure an image of this in her head, from something she had seen on a nature show. She also read that stalls, while not an unheard of situation to encounter, were fairly uncommon in modern aircraft. This in part because modern aircraft, should a plane approach stall conditions, sounds an alarm and the flight control stick automatically shudders. Like anti-lock brakes, she thought. If ignored, the control stick goes further and automatically pushes itself forward and down, pushing the nose down and decreasing the angle of attack. In effect, this action forces the plane, which wants to remain in the air, into stall recovery mode.

♂

From the moment the alarm sounded, Captain Renslow of Flight 3407 overrode the stick pusher, ignored the alarm and the dangerously slow speed, and pulled the controls back and angled the nose up. She watched the animation of the twenty-six seconds of the incident. With its nose thrust stubbornly in the air and at a high angle of attack, the plane pitched, yawed, and spun. The animators had been kind enough not to show the pixelated plane impacting the ground.

⚬

She checked the forecast in Buffalo. Then for no reason at all, she thought of the boyfriend who always drove fast when he was angry, drove fast to let her know that he was angry, and who in the middle of the night in some suburbs made her throw her pot and bowl out the window at high speed before leaving her at a corner 7–11. What an asshole, she said out loud to no one and then, what a wimp. She hated wimps the most. The one before him had been a wimp too. He had called her heart cold. In between there had been a redhead and she wouldn't let him put his face there if he didn't know how, which he didn't. After all three of them there had been a southern redhead, Abigail, who had left no taste but her slow-to-say southern-sounding name.

⚬

She checked the forecast over the Atlantic. She checked the ocean currents, which way the currents moved and how the air moved over them. She read about storms, the months when the weather was particularly volatile. She'd lived through the 1993 "Storm of the Century," a blizzard stretching from Central America to Canada. If her life had been disrupted, she did not recall. She looked for air-turbulence indicators and forecast maps. There were no maps forecasting turbulence though there were maps made of past areas of turbulence. She looked at them but her looking didn't matter. She couldn't read them anyway. All the lines and color gradients, she didn't know what they meant.

♂

She checked the weather in the ITCZ—the Inter Tropical Convergence Zone. The zone wraps around near the equator, give or take some latitude lines, and houses the most volatile weather on the planet. Clouds and storms piled miles high. She reminded herself to tie her shoes tight the next time she boarded a plane. This was recommended.

♂

It is rare for a plane to fall apart in flight. No, she thought, break apart. That's what they called it. Breaking apart mid-flight. Decompression. No, explosive decompression. They said it tore clothes from bodies. Bodies. It was that violent. But it happened rarely, maybe in extreme turbulence or wind shear, when the forces acting on the plane became so great, and the forces only became so great when a plane exceeded its flight envelope, its pre-programmed capacities for speed and altitude. The coffin corner, they called it. An unstable combination of speed and altitude. It involved things she could not understand. Critical mach numbers, gross weight, and G-force loading. She thought that the coffin must refer to the shape that the extremes made on the graph. She thought that when the dots—max altitude, speed, G-force, air going over and under each wing—are all connected by lines, the shape must vaguely resemble a coffin. In the coffin corner, the forces are extreme. On the graph, where it is impossible to keep a plane in stable flight, the lines come together. She wanted to be lazy and blissfully empty. She wanted to be eating a grapefruit by a golf course and tanning.

♂

The last time a plane broke apart, that she knew of, was the Japan Airlines Flight 123 incident in 1985. Not counting incidents where planes collided with each other, it still remains the deadliest airplane accident. She didn't even know that 520 people could fit on an airplane. What a big plane, she thought. It must have been a huge plane. An auditorium of a plane. In 1978 that huge plane had been taking off when the tail of the plane struck the runway—something like clipping a hurdle with your toe. The tail had been nicked. A repair had not conformed to the approved methods. The repaired parts weakened during the take-off and landing cycles, of which there were over ten thousand. Then they broke. There was explosive decompression at cruising altitude and after a remarkable thirty-two minutes of remaining in the air, the plane crashed into rugged mountains. She clicked around. Pressurization cycles were hard on a plane's structure. They weakened parts, caused damage, and weakened damaged parts further. Pressurization cycles require continuous expansion and contraction of the body. Similarly, at O'Hare a plane that had been improperly repaired after a tail strike crashed in the Illinois fields right after takeoff.

♂

Up and down, up and down. The orthopedic surgeon had rolled close to her with a plastic model of a knee that included the kneecap, femur, cartilage, and ligaments. This is what happens to your knee, he said, while making the model knee bend with his hands, every time you lunge. When you go down, the meniscus is compressed by the kneecap. Only your kneecap does not track smoothly over the bone, it goes off to the side, like this. All of this up and down, wearing in the wrong direction, causes swelling and that's what makes your knee hurt. He pointed to the x-ray, the oddly worn shape of her kneecap. They called it Napoleon knee, for the jaunty tri-cornered way the patella was worn down.

♂

Weather, it seemed, was no longer the deciding factor. Between 1964 and 1985, wind shear, or the sudden variation in horizontal and vertical wind velocities, was responsible for a large portion of aviation accidents. Then wind shear detectors were installed on most planes. Now wind shear accidents happen about once every ten years. The modern airplane is built to withstand a great deal. The Wright brothers had to contend with weather conditions. Some days they simply could not take their practical flying machines to the sky.

♂

What are you doing, he asked, as he passed through the room on his way to the kitchen. She quickly clicked away from the injury reports gathered about a downed China Airlines flight and onto the Urban Outfitters website, where she examined socks patterned with, the caption read, authentic Navajo designs. She struggled to catch her breath. Nothing, she said, as he was leaving the room.

♂

Though the Wrights started with a bicycle, the classical model for the airplane has always been wings, always the bird.

♂

She read that exactly twenty-two years to the day after the tail of a China Airlines Boeing 747 had been improperly repaired after a tail strike on the runway, the plane broke apart mid-flight following explosive decompression. She went to a Taiwanese website and downloaded the official report from the Aviation Safety Council. The only event listed under the heading "Sequence of Events" was "Disintegration." There was a list and accompanying diagram of how many people had been found clothed and how many naked according to the assigned seating on the plane. Some bodies were not recovered. Notable to the investigation was how many bodies were found with injuries to only one side or the other. Some were injured only on the left side, some only on the right side. There was no mention of what this might mean, but to someone, once, the details had been significant. Before the people had been turned into paper, she quoted in her head. It was a line from a poem. It mattered once, if only to them. Before they had been turned into paper. She repeated the phrase a few times and then poked at the skin under her thumbnails with a sewing needle, pulling little bits of skin away until she began to bleed. Thirsty, she got up to get a glass of water.

♂

Earlier that year she had been trying to leave Missouri. The plane, the only one at the regional airport, was leaking. From the gate area windows she was belly to the plane and she could see clear liquid running from its underside. It was quick, like water from a gutter, and pooled beneath the plane before catching the cracks and spreading like wires. Hydraulic fluid, she thought. She watched the pilot, in his short-sleeved shirt, circle the plane before coming back into the gate area and announcing that the flight would be delayed. Then he went back out to the plane. She watched as his clearance badge, strung on a lanyard around his neck, bounced over his shoulder as it caught the wind. It was five-thirty in the morning. It was her birthday. The liquid looked almost pretty. The skies were clear. She wondered how long they would be delayed, if it would become partly cloudy. She opened her laptop. She could check the forecast.

♂

She checked the forecast for Missouri. She checked the forecast for the connecting airports. She started to feel like she was in the middle of the country. She checked the forecast for the coast. She had taken some pills to stay calm but their peak effect would be lost while waiting at the gate. She decided to take some more, for good measure, to be prepared. She turned to the gate area television, showing a huge wave washing over—the screen flashed—Japan. Her eyes slid in and out of focus. She thought of how she and her brother used to play in the mud in summer, when they were kids, how they built mud cities with Tonka trucks and Legos. Then, as the afternoon slid out of view, they turned on the hose and washed away all of the bricks and people, some lost for good in the yard. She squinted at the television that was now listing wave arrival times for Hawaii and the California coast. Huh, she said out loud. Confused, she turned her gaze back to the tarmac and sank lower in the chair.

♂

A month later, tornados churned over chunks of Missouri. The weather channel interrupted its regularly scheduled programming. She pulled the ottoman close to the television and turned it up loud. She checked the forecast. It was cloudy everywhere. With her eyes she followed the animated angry red polygons outlining the severe storm cells as they moved across the screen west to east, stopped, recycled, and started again. While she watched, she picked at her toenails. Her toenails were soft and she easily picked them apart. She thought about how quickly she could get to the basement if there was a tornado. When he came home, he looked at the television and said that he didn't want to watch the stuff about the weather. There was a game on.

♂

In some of the dreams the house is an airplane but she doesn't realize it until the plane has already taken off, already started to bank and roll. The flight attendants, when there are any, wear the wide smiles of devils. She always looks around for her parents.

☌

In the days following the lost Air France plane, online forums devoted to aviation were filled with hypotheses. She found several cached conversations among members. Lightning, said some. It was possible. Unlike other planes in the area, the pilots had chosen not to detour around the volatile storms brewing in the equatorial Inter Tropical Convergence Zone, the ITCZ. Catastrophic malfunction, said others. What could cause the total failure of all systems at once. Crazy turbulence, spatial disorientation, and bombs. There could have been an explosion, a bomb. There was doubt expressed as to whether bodies would ever be recovered. One user noted that in the cases of small single-engine aircraft that had pancaked to the ground, the bodies disintegrated, even vaporized, upon impact. Wouldn't that be the case, the user asked, if the plane had hit the water belly first? Would anything but shards of fuselage ever be found? The queries had been made years ago, before the plane and eventually the black box were raised to the surface. The mystery, it turned out, was not really a mystery at all. Just the rules of flight.

☌

Once she had been on her way to work during morning rush hour. It had been hot, very hot, and she wore a strange sheer pullover, lime green, that she never wore, and the dark sunglasses that she preferred so that she could avoid making direct eye contact with others. At the intersection where the curb on the opposite side jutted out, where everyone had to swerve to avoid hitting it, her front wheel struck the curb. There was a bang as the tire deflated with an explosion that rocked her, and then the car fell onto the pavement with another bang and came to a metallic stop. Standing outside the car to wait for the tow truck, she looked at the wheel. The metal rim was crushed. Flattened like a pancake. The wheel was a total loss. She blamed it on the lime green pullover. It was bad luck. Within the hour her body began to stiffen and ache from the jolt.

⚭

She tried numerous query tactics. "Effect of ocean temperature on air currents," "effect of air currents and ocean temperature on air travel, turbulence," "air over the Atlantic," "dangerous flying zones," "turbulence indicators," and "turbulence on transatlantic flights." It was known that the airspeed indicators on the Air France flight had begun malfunctioning shortly before the plane's disappearance. This was fairly common and due to icing of the pitot tubes, which are positioned on the wings, at high altitudes. A pitot tube is a pressure-measurement instrument. Through a complex series of equations involving pressure and fluids, velocity is determined. It is known that the tubes freeze up: ideally they are installed with heating devices to keep the tubes from becoming clogged with ice. Sometimes the tube heating systems don't work. Other times, the pilots fail to turn them on. She read on the internet that failure of the airspeed indicator system or its accompanying heating components could result in catastrophic consequences. There was a list of airplane crashes in which this was the culprit. In the case of a tropical climate crash, it was hypothesized that the tubes had been blocked by nesting wasps, the black and yellow mud dauber, known to build its nests in or on man-made objects. Freezing is a more common cause of blocked tubes, but it is thought that as the plane descends or passes through warmer air, the indicators will return to normal function. The best she could tell was that this was a common and known problem without a direct solution, like failing to wake up from anesthesia after surgery. It just happened. Some companies made better tubes than others. Some airlines replaced the so-so tubes, and others did not. Most airplanes are quite old, she learned.

♂

The FAA strongly recommended that one brand of tubes be replaced with another and, of course, that all consistently faulty tubes be replaced. But it was hard to replace all those tubes on so many planes. After Air France, once people calmed down about it, the issue of the tubes seemed like less and less of an issue. The best tubes were expensive. Bulletins were posted; recommendations were made. She checked her ticket, the itinerary, and the make of the plane. It was impossible to know if the tubes had been replaced on that plane.  She considered tracking down the number of planes in the company fleet, of what type, and their age. She started to search for maintenance records, other bulletins and recommendations, safety reports, documentation of who had followed the recommendations and who hadn't. On Amazon, she could buy the same brand of pitot tube used on airplanes for fifty-six dollars and sixty cents.

⚤

From her brother's apartment in Milan she checked the forecast. She had not brought rain boots. The internet was slow, but she kept up with things going on around the world. It was snowing back home. She wondered if that would keep up. She thought of the regional airport, wondering if the jets were cold and lonely at night. Though she no longer remembered where or when, she had been on a plane and it was cold and the pilot was doing his outside check of the plane in short sleeves. She knew that pilots were required to visually inspect the plane from a 360-degree walk-around. As he'd walked by the wing, he'd reached up and, with his hand, had tenderly brushed off the light coat of snow. The wing sparkled. Her brother asked her something about Japan. She said she didn't know for sure. Radiation was leaking from the nuclear plants that had been damaged by the wave. Accurate reports were hard to find, and when found, were too technical to understand. Tokyo was being tight-lipped and cagey about the situation. She studied the aerial photographs of the damage. It was, they said, extensive. It looked it. The front page of the news ran a story about Libya. There was unrest. Some called it civil war. Her brother was glad she had come. He offered her a small cup of Italian coffee, which she accepted.

♂

There was trouble in Tripoli. In the back of her mind she recalled that the news made much of Libya for its bizarre head of state. The Italians had opinions on Libya, as the two countries were in close contact. She asked her brother if there were a lot of Libyans in Italy. Yes, he said. Lots of Libyans, lots of Arabs, lots of immigrants from everywhere. Not everyone thought immigration was a good idea. Xenophobia, he said, it's affecting all of Europe. People aren't so nice to me anymore, he said. But you can still get good falafel, he said, if you know where to look. She examined the headlines, the photos of the Libyan leader, Muammar Gaddafi. She thought his hair looked like an unfinished Jheri curl. It was suspected that he had personally ordered the bombing of Pan Am Flight 103, also known as the Lockerbie bombing, named for the spot above the earth where the plane had exploded and where people on the ground had been killed. There was a complex and obscure reason for the bombing of the plane, to which the individual passengers could not have made the slightest connection. The bomb had been inside a suitcase with baby clothes purchased in Malta. When it exploded, it punched a twenty-inch hole in the fuselage. She read that this alone had not brought down the plane. On occasion, holes opened in a fuselage due to weakened stress points and planes were able to fly, more or less normally, and then land without incident. The Lockerbie plane broke apart as the result of resounding shock waves emanating from the point of explosion, shock waves that ricocheted along the length of the fuselage and then back towards the point of explosion where they collided with the initial shockwaves, still emanating.

⚲

Plastic explosives and timers were not something the Wright brothers could have foreseen. She imagined that their initial fascination had been something simple. A bird. Birds, they must have known, did not stall. She imagined that the Wrights had been in it for the sheer joy of the thing.

⚲

She began to see Gaddafi everywhere. Gaddafi at the markets, Gaddafi wandering the Palazzo Reale, Gaddafi at the crepe shop, Gadaffi at H&M. After a day of sightseeing, she headed back uptown from the Duomo where, she thought, was a good place to plant a bomb. Enormous crowds, no metal detectors or body scanners. On the train she swore she was sitting across from a Gaddafi in tight-fitting jeans and a shiny jacket. She stared at the man. He looked intently at his cell phone. She recalled that cell phones could be transmitters, detonation devices. A tinny woman's voice announced the stops as they approached. *Brenta. Firmata Brenta.*

♂

Maybe people who were preparing to blow up other people did not appear nervous. She imagined that such a task must take a certain kind of calm. People blew up trains all the time, didn't they? They had in London, and in Madrid. There had been bombings. And people continued as if there was nothing to it. Sometimes the Tube got bombed. People became pink mist. It happened. Work went on. Cleanup crews were called in, the stock exchanges reopened. Or he could be setting off a bomb placed elsewhere, like in the crowded plaza at the Duomo. Hadn't she read that there was some deep antagonism between Italy and Libya? Something originating, maybe, from the time of Mussolini? Hadn't she read that? The man looked like he was trying to place a call. She decided that he looked nothing like Gadaffi, that neither he nor his cell phone were real.

♂

The tallest and most aggressive mountain ranges lie beneath the ocean. In the area where Air France Flight 447 went down, the news kept repeating that "razor sharp" peaks had hampered the recovery efforts. Razor. She said it out loud, letting her teeth clench and grind over the r's. It would take years, millions of dollars, and blame shifted from one foot to the other before the plane was eventually found, some parts intact, some bodies still strapped in the seats. The most common image flashed on the news websites was that of a wheel assembly buried deep in the sand of the ocean floor. The only light shining on it that of the camera taking the picture. The ghostly blue image reminded her of pictures of the Titanic when the ship had been found. This was like the Titanic, she thought, only any joy in finding the plane was seriously muted. There was no clapping. The Titanic had been a labor of love, not an inquiry. Relatives of the crash victims were torn. Some wanted the bodies to remain at sea, others wanted them raised. Everyone wanted an explanation. In the end, the explanation was simple. Confused by the malfunctioning airspeed indicators, the pilots disregarded the stall warning that sounded no fewer than seventy-two times. After all, they must have known that it was difficult, if not impossible, to stall such a sophisticated and modern airplane, a plane that practically flew itself. St. Elmo's fire, visible from the cockpit, appeared on the wings. For the entire minute and twenty-six seconds of the final event, the co-pilot pulled back on the controls and unwittingly flew the plane into the ocean.

☌

The Wright brothers had been deeply convinced that with practice, a flying machine could be controlled and made practical. They had started with bicycles on the prairies of Indiana. She thought of the bicycle and it made sense. The way it wobbled at first but then, with speed, synced with body and road. She remembered riding by the square fields, the mesmerizing heat of summer, the hypnotic turn of the wheel as she looked down. The tar bubbling in the heat, the wheels popping the bubbles. Every now and then the light wind would blow over the green fields and blow dampness onto her skin.

♂

Over tea and dry biscuits her brother mentioned that radiation from Japan's damaged reactors was predicted to reach California via air. How do they know, she asked, if it is Japan's radiation and not someone else's? Besides, she said, she had read that the amount of radiation one is subjected to from living near a coal-burning power plant was much greater than that of living near a nuclear power plant, or the parts-per-billion increase that sources claimed to be detecting over the ocean on the air's way to California. It's the rural Pennsylvanians and West Virginians, she said, who have to worry. They are getting radiated all the time. She searched the internet for when the radiation was supposed to reach the east coast. Many of the first men to discover the ability to harness nuclear power and radiation had died of radiation poisoning, just as the first physician to identity SARS, the especially deadly pneumonia that struck China in 2003, died soon after alerting the world. Like many others, he had begun feeling feverish on a plane. She went back to checking the forecast. It was snowing back home, and cold. She hoped it was not snowing when she landed. She tried to envision herself back in her house. It was better, she knew, than envisioning the delicate sensors becoming blocked with ice, each individual crystal humming with icy uniqueness. She saw the gray carpet on the stairs, the flecks of autumn's leaves ground in by boot heels and the assemblies of dust on the white wooden molding. The first thing she would do when she arrived, she decided, would be to pass her dust mop over the floors. Every now and then, she came across more footage of the waves. The soundless aerial video of minivans trying to outrun the water only to be overtaken and tossed. They bobbed about like bath toys or buoys. She always clicked away from these videos. The only safe place to be was in a plane.

## The gunslinger neuron

Everyone should get in touch with their inner fate

of snow afflicted by a bad case of the doldrums.

Reader, I would not live in a powderless tree: If I could

I would align myself with the powerscape.

At times I practice being sad in the mirror.

I practice a blister. My murder face.

Of what I remind myself I am not sure.

Some calypso in the distance.

Beakers of candid morning.

A snow cannot be a lie.

On a raft in the ocean

looking towards a blue

iceberg I am Look! I tell

him as I paddle toward

it. How bluing the water!

I want him to see how

bluing the ice. But he is

not here when I look

over my shoulder, my

good shoulder, and my

good shoulder tells me

the current is taking us

toward the windless

night! This is my last

night in the nest. I turn

to tell him but he is not

here, how frightening!

That the water should

turn so cold now that the

current drifts and all my

possessions are on this

raft. The glittery iceberg

now not at all what I

thought

Though possessing no skill
I grew a horn from my head. Say
despite himself every beloved boy
goldens properly. I reach for his
soft metal to make it a rock star
but in me he grew *who's that*,
praxis & frisson. The meridian
automatic in my clench, my thrills.
It may well be real. Suddenly
from my every layer
                    horns grew themselves.

Now that mine has gone bad I am glad for the new heart that departed from one body, was held in hands and lowered into the walls of my sunless cradle never meant to feel air then sealed with a scar I worry some about the scar, if the sutures are sloppy, if the surgeon will fall asleep but to protect the new heart from a lymphatic counterattack the surgeon wraps the heart in a papier-mâché of dollar bills to be washed away by the currents of blood over the years until just the red heart remains happy to be alive until I am happy to be awake and alive and so so rich

To carve the atria of the heart

    into a face

    you use the sternum saw

to split the breastbone,

    window the heart

and then the incisors of the meadow vole

    meant for light grasses and barks,

to render the bi and tricuspid shapes.

    When he leans in close to please

       the writhing in my ghost

the entirety of his tree shakes like a palm

    slapping the earth,

shaken by the instrument necessary

not to feel alive

    —but to be alive


    is an instrument of injury,

involuntary tissue pummeled to open, close.

I bite off my tongue to

keep the illness from

spreading its ugly baby.

To tie off what remains I

twist the end tight as a

sausage. I tuck the bitten

off piece into my cheek

pocket and take it with

me. How difficult it is to

talk! But I can still

maneuver the tongue

muscle stump. I go to

the waiting car.

　　　　My job is to

make others do what they

would rather not do and

the driver does not want

to go where I had asked

him to take me. So I

open my mouth and let

my tonguepiece unfurl

its swarm. How difficult

it is to talk! But see? He

still understands what I

mean. How bright the

midday sun as the car

pulls away from the

curb.

**My heart is full of practical folklore**

hold water in your mouth
    to keep from crying
when cutting an onion
    to keep from crying hold water
to cut the water hold the onion
    in your mouth to keep from crying
when crying hold water
    to keep from cutting
the onion in your mouth
    to hold water keep cutting
the onion when in your mouth
    hold the crying in your mouth
when cutting the onion
    cut an onion in your mouth
to keep from crying in the water
    when cutting an onion
hold water in your mouth
    to keep from crying

It is said that what follows cannot be proven.

"Like a barn came up and smack smacked me"

that's Midwest.

Or disproven. They called it

year of the cyclone. Year of the unmistakable

red wolves of vortex.

Hook echo an unmistakable

signature.

They declared it the year of life, which considering all the deaths

was remarkable.

The buzzards, some chartreuse, some with new "green" condos.

The buzzards came resurrecting their wealth.

Resurrecting that arcane practice

of becoming whatever they thought they were worth.

It was remarkable.

The town came back bearing the mark of a saber.

A motion, as in a sweep-sweep, only broken by its trigger.

Or swollen mitts of tigers.

Or clothes, with dancing lit

dancing second only to the pollen.

*Homo narrans* (sustenance)[1]

---

[1] No one is sure why but the cities fall in on themselves. Some whisper *quake*, but this is not a grinding or a shudder, just a fall. Buildings kill everyone inside. There is no rescue effort. After a time the streets are quiet and the rest of us become very lonely. No one knows how to begin looking for the people we knew existed. Where is my friend, the social worker? To get anywhere we walk or swim. After a time, we can stitch our own rucksacks and rope together dogs to pull sleds when the snow begins. It still snows. For sustenance we drink the leftover wax from votives, melted and stirred with a twist of honey. In the beginning we are amazed at how well our insides accept this.

**With a candle for a head**

Wanting to be fit

with something festive.

A high pulse.

To talk all the wrong talk

I had a mouth the way a human has a mouth.

But I was a dune of coal.

The street yawned its long sheath peeled open like a wire

in the night.

I went down to the cornerfull of black mist,

the station of a fragment human.

It began there in leather cuffs of light.

I thought I did not exist. Or I was a team of people.

I wanted expert protection.

I wanted something crazier. A high skying flyover.

Some William Tell.

This time I call out to him by
name from inside the elevator
that rattles downward as it
goes it grows smaller and
hotter and fills with stale as I
press the red button for help
and it does not work but into I
speak and say *save me* exactly
what I believe I mean

I see I've ripped your throat open.


That my life could be better without me.


Like the teratoma whose nails will not stop growing

my life gnaws at me.


That is, I've ripped your throat open with my mouth.


I was staring into the hazy no-see-um nightmusk

with dreams of being a runaway Hollywood boy.

I saw my starlet self clear as television. I changed my name to nightjar.

This sense I have of my past

is not a sense of a past at all.

My soul reads death. I can hardly call to the call of others.

I do not know the names of names you know.

My wrists refuse the train to the desert.

Can you not see through the stillish pool to see

I am trying to believe myself grave.

I will west enough to feather and hibernate where your throat can keep your throat geometry.

No teeth to tear with and heart stilled to skull: the common-brown poorwill

torpors beneath rocks for months.

In the manner of an owl I eject the indigestible parts.

At the top of the hill in the forest at night we are standing face to face as the moon wavers behind a small cloud and when I say no to the baby he pulls a gun and shoots me in the stomach. I hold in what I can and stumble home to my mother. She tries to call for help but keeps fumbling the telephone buttons. Her fingers keep missing. My lips tingle to a numbing

at the top of the hill in the forest at night we are standing face to face as the moon wanders behind a cloud and when I say no to the baby he pulls a gun and shoots me in the stomach. I hold in what I can and stumble home to my mother. She tries to call for help but each time her fingers fumble and miss, fumble and miss.

Warbling

    a thigh appears.  ♂

        The harangue of migration on spent

inverted air. No last gasp

    no point to the land
    beyond the land
    that was the land scrapped.

No margin of then it was here, whole       ♂

    ♂    then not.

        Beyond the horizon    a cancer    ∞    on the horizon

        greedy nucleotide sums.

Another thigh.  ♂

Surely someone's compared *thigh*
to *seashore*. It comes as luscious.
Its luscious as lapping. Its lapping waves.

From the body: like a seller

splits from its house: vulva. sack. junk.


So we read the prehistoric tidings.


Nothing hidden in the flesh


but the bone eating its way out.


♂ ♂

**_Homo narrans_ (do it like this)**

I crisscross the stacks
        searching for my mother
& father. The librarian
        tells me they boarded
the other plane
        that already took off.
This library is an airplane
        I do not want to be on
but the doors are locked
        and _in fact_
the librarian states,
        _we too have taken off._
_See, you didn't feel_
        _a thing._ Her smile
is wide. The etched outlines
        of plump cornfields
slide out of view
        as the books slip
their shelves. The librarian
        instructs us
to look forward,
        hold our arms
overhead like children on a roller
        coaster. Her smile
widens from forehead
        to jaw. She demonstrates
as the plane pitches, yaws
        & dives. _Watch me._ She says,
_See? Do it like this._

.

The poems called "Legends like this I keep keeping" are for Anne Marie Rooney.

"Music for monsters: a curtal sonnet" is for Steve Davenport.

Thanks to the late Jake Adam York for believing in "Forecast."

## Acknowledgments

Thank you to the editors of these publications for publishing poems from this collection, sometimes in earlier versions.

*Barn Owl Review:* "Homo narrans (sustenance)"

*B O D Y Literature:* "Homo narrans (chainsaw)," "Homo narrans (do it like this)," and "Homo narrans (turkey)"

*Copper Nickel:* "Forecast"

*phantom limb:* "Year of the cyclone"

*Southern Indiana Review:* selections from "Cerebrum corpus monstrum"

*Sou'wester:* selections from "Cerebrum corpus monstrum" and "Homo narrans (transplant)"

*Spoon River Poetry Review:* "Crypsisssssssssssssssssssssssssssssssssssssssss"

*The Winter Anthology:* "With a candle for a head"

## Other Books from Tupelo Press

*Fasting for Ramadan: Notes from a Spiritual Practice* (memoir), Kazim Ali

*Another English: Anglophone Poems from Around the World* (anthology), edited by Catherine Barnett and Tiphanie Yanique

*Pulp Sonnets* (poems, with drawings by Amin Mansouri), Tony Barnstone

*Brownwood* (poems), Lawrence Bridges

*Everything Broken Up Dances* (poems), James Byrne

*One Hundred Hungers* (poems), Lauren Camp

*New Cathay: Contemporary Chinese Poetry* (anthology), edited by Ming Di

*Calazaza's Delicious Dereliction* (poems), Suzanne Dracius, translated by Nancy Naomi Carlson

*Gossip and Metaphysics: Russian Modernist Poetry and Prose* (anthology), edited by Katie Farris, Ilya Kaminsky, and Valzhyna Mort

*Poverty Creek Journal* (lyric memoir), Thomas Gardner

*My Immaculate Assassin* (novel), David Huddle

*Darktown Follies* (poems), Amaud Jamaul Johnson

*Dancing in Odessa* (poems), Ilya Kaminsky

*A God in the House: Poets Talk About Faith* (interviews), edited by Ilya Kaminsky and Katherine Towler

*Third Voice* (poems), Ruth Ellen Kocher

*Cooking with the Muse* (cookbook, with poetry anthology), Myra Kornfeld and Stephen Massimilla

*Phyla of Joy* (poems), Karen An-hwei Lee

*A Camouflage of Specimens and Garments* (poems), Jennifer Militello

*Marvels of the Invisible* (poems), Jenny Molberg

*Yes Thorn* (poems), Amy Munson

*Lucky Fish* (poems), Aimee Nezhukumatathil

*The Ladder* (poems), Alan Michael Parker

*Ex-Voto* (poems), Adélia Prado, translated by Ellen Doré Watson

*Why Don't We Say What We Mean?* (essays), Lawrence Raab

*Intimate: An American Family Photo Album* (hybrid memoir), Paisley Rekdal

*Walking Backwards* (poems), Lee Sharkey

*Wintering* (poems), Megan Snyder-Camp

*Swallowing the Sea* (essays), Lee Upton

*Butch Geography* (poems), Stacey Waite

See our complete list at www.tupelopress.org

Printed in the USA
CPSIA information can be obtained
at www.ICGtesting.com
LVHW070355220624
783518LV00003B/3